MW00805941

Reviews

"Coach Simpson's Gun T Offensive Overview is an excellent offensive resource. This course provides the foundation of Coach Simpson's offensive philosophy. Coach believes in the monikers that "Less is More" and the "Rule of 3", which both were evident in the explanation of the offense. His explanations were clear and concise, and the presentations were easy to follow."

Todd Knipp

"This is absolutely amazing. Coach Simpson does an excellent job of explaining his system. Whether you're a young coach or an experienced coach this is must see. You can easily see why he is a successful coach. His detailed organization is on point and I cannot wait to learn more from Coach Simpson."

Mike Kloes

"I've been following coach Simpson for a while now and it's very clear to me that even though I may not be a HC, we have similar philosophies. If you are a Wing T guy looking for ways to "Modernize" your offense, or a Spread guy looking for an effective and efficient run game this is the offense you should be looking at!"

Coach Sheffer

"Most offensive systems you must have really good players to run them, but with Coach Simpson's 'Gun-T' RPO system, you can be very successful just manipulating defenses with the X's & O's." –

Steven Swinson, Indiana Weslyian University

 # Reviews

"Coach Simpson's Gun-T Offense is dynamic and efficient. This course gets into the foundation of building blocks of the Gun-T offense and what you are trying to do offensively to be as successful as possible."

Austin Pink

"As a first year head coach and a first time offensive play caller, I don't know where we would have been without the material that coach Simpson has available. We went from 4-6 to 7-4, to the third round of the postseason, and earned the second best record in school history. The program hadn't been to, nor won a playoff game since 2015. Thank you coach Simpson."

Mike Granato, Head Football Coach, West Orange High School, Florida

"Coach Simpson does an awesome job explaining his system, and he does it a way that people like myself who are not familiar with RPOs can understand!"

Coach Coleman

"As a traditional wing T coach for over 30 years I was looking for a package to add to my offense in order to force defense's to defend width and depth. Coach Simpson's Gun-T RPO offense does exactly that with the built in "what if then" RPO's and RRO's."

Coach Brissette

"The Gun T RPO System really helped us evolve our wing T offense and really put defenses in conflict. This system helped us break a 20 game losing streak and finish with a winning record for the first time since 2014."

Tom Mulligan, Head Coach Elmwood Park High School, Elmwood Park, New Jersey

 # Table of Contents

Acknowledgements -   8

Background -   9

Introduction -   10

Theory -   11

Personnel -   12

RPO Game -   18

Calling Plays -   19

Formations -   21

Motions/Shifts -   41

Plays -   47

Practice Organization -   118

Installation -   122

Tempo -   129

Coaching Staff Organization -   130

Conclusion -   132

About the Author -   134

Acknowledgments

I am a big fan of "system" offenses, from the Tony Franklin System to the Rick Stewart System. Along my journey I have purchased both of their systems to help me learn how an offense functioned. In my opinion, offenses should flow and not be simply plays that are run. By coming up with a systematic approach things just seem to make sense.

I learned the game from these coaches and others that have been willing to give back to others. I did not understand how much time and effort it takes to put together a system that is simple to understand and teach until I started putting my own together. Massive amounts of time go into it, so I want to thank all the coaches that are willing to "put themselves out there" for the coaching community.

I also want to thank all the coaches that have worked with me as we have come up with our own system that we believe in and love. From Gregg Baker, who introduced me to the Wing T system to Jon Johnston who helped me see the spread game, I've worked with coaches that have taught me nuggets along the way. This has helped me create this system, and I would not be where I am without their influence.

The administration and community at all of my schools has been unbelievable. While it has been a process, I have loved every year I have spent coaching and growing this system.

Most importantly I want to thank my players. They are why I coach and while I love the "X's and O's", I love the relationships way more. While I hope to have helped mentor them, they have all influenced me as well. As a coach, never forget the reason we became coaches...the players.

Background

The **Gun T RPO** system is the best of 3 worlds:

The **Wing-T** offensive system has been around for many years. The best part of the Wing-T is the run game that utilizes angles and takes advantage of the defensive alignment by creating them. The Wing-T is also known for its "series" based offense, which has multiple plays that look the same in the backfield action.

The **RPO** system has taken football by storm over the last couple of decades. To be able to place defenders in "conflict" with the run/pass option game gives the offense a numbers advantage at all times. This system is also great because while it seems the quarterback must make a decision on each play, it also "shrinks" his world by having him read only one or two defenders.

The **Power-Spread** game is gaining steam throughout every level of football. To be in the shotgun, but still have a downhill running game is deadly and difficult to defend. Utilizing tight ends and H-backs has become "new" again in football. The reality is this system has been around for awhile, just not in the shotgun.

When combined into the **Gun T RPO** system, these worlds at first seem at odds with one another. However, after a deeper dig, these offenses are all concept based that build in answers to handle any defense that may show up on a given day.

When I first "stepped into the deep end" by putting my offensive system out there, I was overwhelmed by the support from the coaching community. I have attempted to continue to build on this offensive system each season. This book will give some guidance to how we would install this at our youth levels.

Introduction

I, like most coaches, have worked hard to listen to people I respect and attempt to take little nuggets from those willing to give. Now, I have the opportunity to give back and I hope this offensive system can be of help to you in your journey as a coach. Feel free to take any part of this offense that can help you, but I feel what makes it work is the entire system. We have worked hard to continue to grow it and work through the problems that can come from blending different worlds.

The entire system can be found on Coachtube.com:

There is also more information on my website:

There is no magic pill. When we watch the game of football there are champions that run a variety of offensive systems. I would point out that those who seem to have the most success have a belief in their offense. Most have worked hard to go over as many "if-then" situations and build in answers. I am no different. I wanted to create an offense that would work against any coverage, any front or any blitz package the defense might throw at us. While the game is won and lost with the players on the field, I wanted to be sure to give my players every advantage I could.

I hope this guide will help you as you work with your younger athletes, but realize that simply having good plays will not guarantee success, work with your athletes and teach the true concepts of the offense. Also, be sure to remember you are there to mentor the next generation. Take that role seriously.

Theory

This offense operates with what I call the "rule of three". We attempt to limit the areas of the field we attack into three concepts or less. In this playbook you will see:

3 strong side run plays
3 quick side run plays
3 flood concepts
2 play action concepts
3 screen concepts
3 RPO concepts

Simple is the key in this offense. We want to just "tag" each run, screen, RPO or flood concept to take advantage of the defense. Then when you mix in some motion and formations, it becomes much more difficult for a defense. The main objective is to only use a motion/formation/tag for a specific purpose, not simply to look complex. If they are not stopping your base plays, don't stop yourself by calling something else!

In this guide I will go through the plays I'd implement for youth teams. Understand that any offense MUST change to highlight the players. This offense can be run under-center and it can be run without the RPO element. Adapt to what your personnel dictates.

I hope this system can serve as a basis for your offense. It can be run in its "pure" form, or many coaches add their own wrinkles to fit their athletes. The goal of all offenses should be to fit our players.

Theory

At the youth level we usually start with the rule of 1. Can we become proficient at 1 concept before moving on? The hardest part of working with younger athletes is have them understand that we must be great at the basic fundamentals before scheme really matters.

As a youth coach, your practices should be focused on working the fundamentals with your athletes more than simply scrimmaging. This goes for installing this offense as well. Buck sweep is a great play, but if you do not teach your line the basic rules and practice with them individually on down blocking or pull kicking, it will not work.

I have plenty of additional resources if you'd like more help with the offensive line, but the goal for me in this book was to provide the overview and how I would adjust this offense for the youth level.

It would be wise to visit with all the youth coaches and the high school coaches to see what needs to be installed at which level. Constant communication is key to a great program.

Personnel Choices

When you are designing any offense it should always adapt and evolve to your players skill set. While I love certain plays, each season our "best" play rotates depending on what our personnel looks like. Working with scheme is fun, but football is not played on a whiteboard and your "X's" may be better or worse than their "O's" at certain skills. The great offensive coaches are always able to highlight the skill set of their players and hide their deficiencies as much as possible.

In this section, I will give you the "optimal" skills each position has. Understand that if you do not have each position, you can still run the system, but I'd recommend highlighting specific parts. I refer to a few of those in the "IF-THEN" section later in this book.

As a coach be sure to constantly evaluate your players and find their strengths. In the Gun-T RPO system there are multiple spots that can have different skill sets, but a few key ones that you want to place your "better" players. This portion is my guide to helping play players at the position they will have the most success. Each team must decide for themselves who goes where, but this will at least describe the theory.

Personnel Choices

When running this offense there are a few "non-negotiable" parts you absolutely must have. But most of the time there are player with the required skills at each position. As I mentioned in a prior chapter, as coaches we must adapt our offense to the players we have. That being said, there are a few qualities you should search for at each position.

Quarterback - This is the key to your offense. Ideally, this position would be a dual threat. While not everyone has that option, he must be at least able to pull the ball from time to time. The offense will drastically adapt to his skill set. If he is a thrower, it has multiple passing schemes/play action and of course RPO plays. If he is a runner, there are several designed runs for him and the ability to go Empty is a must in today's game.

In short, find your best athlete if possible that can handle the pressure of playing QB and adapt to what he does well. If given the option, I've always deferred to the guy that can run the ball and use his legs over a traditional QB. However, you can be successful with both.

Personnel Choices

F - This should be your best athlete. By design this position will touch the ball the most of any spot (except the QB position). It is easy to get them the ball in space (empty/screens) or simply run the ball (buck/belly). As with every position, you must adapt to their skill set, but this needs to be your best player.

B - This is the hardest position to find and the most important one. It will cause you to adjust what you do offensively to fit his skill set. I would attempt to find your second-best player if he is able/willing to block and put him in this position. Size will matter at this spot, since he will be asked to down block defensive ends and linebackers. If he is gritty, but undersized, there are some adjustments that can be made, but he must be effective at blocking.

The second part of his job is as important. We want this player to be a good runner – if he is very athletic, we will run jet and counter with him. He also needs to be able to catch at least short passes or play action passes. In my opinion, other than the QB, this position will dictate how much you use certain formations and plays.

Personnel Choices

A – A traditional slot WR. Often for us this is our third RB or an undersized WR. Can get him the ball on multiple concepts and even hand him the ball if you need to.

X – Traditional WR. Depending on what you have available this position can be utilized often, or not much.

Y – Tight-end. Must be able to block defensive lineman. His job is crucial on buck. We generally pick our 3rd guard for this spot. If he has the ability to catch the ball that is great, but he must be a willing and able blocker for this offense to work.

QG – Most important lineman on the team. He needs to be your most athletic player on the line. Size is secondary. He will be pulling on almost all strong side runs. When you decide who goes where, start at this position.

SG – Second most important lineman on the team. He will pull kick most of the time, but needs to be athletic enough to wrap for Quick Belly. Usually the stronger, not as athletic of the two guards.

QT – Next most important lineman. What his skill set brings to the table will allow you (or not) to run to the quick side and all your RPO game on the backside. He also needs to be able to get in space on screens and get to second level on RPO game.

C – Must be very consistent at snapping for the offense to run smoothly. Usually this is a smart kid that can call the fronts and is able to handle backside blocking. If he is not as great a blocker, we can give help, but if he is a solid blocker it makes the scheme much easier to achieve.

ST – Usually this is a very physical, but not as athletic tackle. Often for us this is our biggest lineman. If he played at the college level he would have to play guard since often these types of bodies struggle with speed. Must be able to down block, double team and cut/hinge on backside runs.

Youth Choices

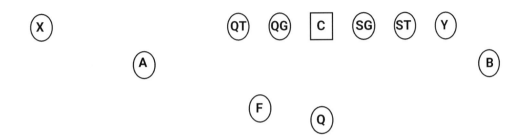

While each coach must make certain adjustments (especially at the youth level) it is important to make sure that the guards in this offense are the best offensive linemen – usually they will be athletes that could almost play running back or linebacker.

Do not simply pick the best arm for the QB position. This spot needs to be an athlete that shows leadership skills as well as an ability to process information quickly. Bodies will change as young men grow up.

At the youth level I would play the best athlete at the "F" position, followed by the "B" position.

Strong-Quick

We run a QUICK and STRONG SIDE
--We rarely have 5-6 good offensive linemen

--We wanted to have spots for guys that were too slow for traditional Wing-T spots

This also makes our line only learn plays one way
--Easier to install plays

--More time to work on types of blocks each specific position uses

--IE -- Strong tackles NEVER PULL or REACH in our system

RPO Overview

R.P.O. stands for Run-Pass-Option. In this offense the "R" comes first. We are trying to protect our base run game by supplying answers to problems. The RPO portion of the offense is to build-in answers to protect the running game. This offense has 1st/2nd/3rd level RPO's. My suggestion to those of you new to this portion of the game would be to start with 1st level RPO's, slowly progress to 2nd, and then possibly 3rd level RPO's.

The beauty of the RPO game is that you can attach the SAME RPO concepts to the entire running game series. Once the quarterback learns the read he can work it on buck sweep or strong belly. Each of our RPO's is built to address problem areas. We want to have very quick concepts we can go to in the middle of a game.

The RPO section is put in with Buck Sweep and Strong Belly and will give you simple RPO concepts that affect the least amount of players (generally the quick tackle and backside players). This allows the offense to become very good at the base run plays with minimal time spent on the backside adjustments.

*If you are coaching a young team, I'd highly suggest limiting RPO's to Screens and QB run game. You may even install the runs without any RPO's and come back to teach them later. It is better to get great at simple concepts and slowly add than to do too much at one time.

Calling Plays

Play call from the coach to the players will follow this format:

1- Formation (+any tags)
2 - Any motion/shift
3 - Run Concept (+any tags)
4 - RPO Play side
5 - RPO Back side

These can get wordy if you run multiple movements and RPO's on each side, but many plays can be just three words. The only player who needs to learn the entire call is the quarterback. Most of the players will only be listening for part of the call or the tags. Here are some examples of play calls:

Red - Buck - Fast

This would be in our strong right (Red) formation. The run play is buck sweep. The wide receivers are running a fast screen.

Blue Flop - Train - Buck - Bubble

This would be our strong left formation (Blue) and our "A" would split out to the other side (Flop). Train is the motion call for "A" so he would come in motion behind the QB. The play would be buck sweep. The wide receivers (A) would be running a bubble screen.

Red - Bus - Jet

This would be strong right formation (Red). Our "B' would come in motion. The run play is jet sweep. Since there is no RPO attached, we don't need to tag it.

Calling Plays

Red Lion - Quick Belly - 42 Fast

This would be a strong right formation (Red) and our "B" would go to make it trips left (Lion). The run play is quick belly. The screen would go to our #2 WR in the trips (42 fast).

Blue - Fly - Q Buck - Bubble

This would be strong left formation (Blue) and our "F" would motion to the quick side (Fly). The run play is quarterback (Q) buck sweep. The RPO would be a bubble (by rule our most inside player runs the bubble, so our "F").

*As you can see throughout this playbook it will be filled with our base run and pass concepts. But you can be as creative as possible. If I listed every possibility this playbook could easily be well over 400-pages.

*At the youth level I would stick to a formation and motion at most before running a play. Or a formation and an RPO if you QB can handle this.

Formations

 # Alignment Rules

A few general rules for alignment:

Y and X are always on the line of scrimmage to make sure each formation is legal

A, B and F are the "moveable" pieces and are always off the ball

Quick side goes away from the call and **strong** side always goes to the call.

 # Formation Install

While each team is different here is the general guideline we use when installing formations:

3rd grade – Red/Blue (possibly Flop)
4th grade – Red/Blue, Flop, Trips
5th grade – Red/Blue, Flop, Trips, Empty
6th grade – As much as they can handle, without confusing athletes

Again – each coach must do what their athletes can handle, but in my experience, it is best to become strong at 1-2 formations at a young age. Most youth defenses will not change much as the game progresses, and this will allow your athletes to understand blocking schemes as the game goes on. Do not simply change formations for the sake of changing formations.

Red

Ⓧ　　　　　ⓆT ⓆG □C ⓈG ⓈT Ⓨ

　　　Ⓐ　　　　　　　　　　　　Ⓑ

　　　　　Ⓕ　　Ⓠ

Position	Alignment
X	Top of the numbers
A	Split X and QT off the ball
F	Heels on QB toes. Split the QG and QT
Y	Head even with hip of center. 2 ft splits
B	2x2 off Y
QT	Head even with hip of center. 2 ft splits
QG	Head even with hip of center. 2 ft splits
C	On Ball
SG	Head even with hip of center. 2 ft splits
ST	Head even with hip of center. 2 ft splits
Q	Heels at 5 yards

Blue

Ⓨ ⓈⓉ ⓈⒼ ☐C ⓆⒼ ⓆⓉ ⓧ

Ⓑ Ⓐ

Ⓕ

Ⓠ

Position	Alignment
X	Top of the numbers
A	Split X and QT off the ball
F	Heels on QB toes. Split the QG and QT
Y	Head even with hip of center. 2 ft splits
B	2x2 off Y
QT	Head even with hip of center. 2 ft splits
QG	Head even with hip of center. 2 ft splits
C	On Ball
SG	Head even with hip of center. 2 ft splits
ST	Head even with hip of center. 2 ft splits
Q	Heels at 5 yards

Red
Flop

Position	Alignment
X	Top of the numbers
A	**On numbers to the strong side**
F	Heels on QB toes. Split the QG and QT
Y	Head even with hip of center. 2 ft splits
B	2x2 off Y
QT	Head even with hip of center. 2 ft splits
QG	Head even with hip of center. 2 ft splits
C	On Ball
SG	Head even with hip of center. 2 ft splits
ST	Head even with hip of center. 2 ft splits
Q	Heels at 5 yards

Blue
Flop

Y ST SG C QG QT   X

A   B

Q   F

Position	Alignment
X	Top of the numbers
A	**On numbers to strong side**
F	Heels on QB toes. Split the QG and QT
Y	Head even with hip of center. 2 ft splits
B	2x2 off Y
QT	Head even with hip of center. 2 ft splits
QG	Head even with hip of center. 2 ft splits
C	On Ball
SG	Head even with hip of center. 2 ft splits
ST	Head even with hip of center. 2 ft splits
Q	Heels at 5 yards

Red
Empty

X   QT   QG   C   SG   ST   Y

     A   F   B

           Q

Position	Alignment
X	Top of the numbers
A	Split X and QT off the ball
F	**Split A and QT off the ball**
Y	Head even with hip of center. 2 ft splits
B	2x2 off Y
QT	Head even with hip of center. 2 ft splits
QG	Head even with hip of center. 2 ft splits
C	On Ball
SG	Head even with hip of center. 2 ft splits
ST	Head even with hip of center. 2 ft splits
Q	Heels at 5 yards

Blue
Empty

Y   ST   SG   C   QG   QT   X

B   F   A

Q

Position	Alignment
X	Top of the numbers
A	Split X and QT off the ball
F	**Split A and QT off the ball**
Y	Head even with hip of center. 2 ft splits
B	2x2 off Y
QT	Head even with hip of center. 2 ft splits
QG	Head even with hip of center. 2 ft splits
C	On Ball
SG	Head even with hip of center. 2 ft splits
ST	Head even with hip of center. 2 ft splits
Q	Heels at 5 yards

Red
Lion

X   QT   QG   C   SG   ST   Y

A   B

F

Q

Position	Alignment
X	Top of the numbers
A	Split X and QT off the ball
F	Heels on QB toes. Split the QG and QT
Y	Head even with hip of center. 2 ft splits
B	**Split A and QT off the ball**
QT	Head even with hip of center. 2 ft splits
QG	Head even with hip of center. 2 ft splits
C	On Ball
SG	Head even with hip of center. 2 ft splits
ST	Head even with hip of center. 2 ft splits
Q	Heels at 5 yards

Blue
Roar

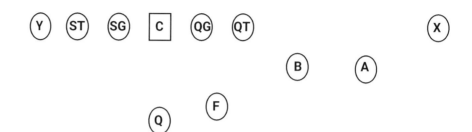

Position	Alignment
X	Top of the numbers
A	Split X and QT off the ball
F	Heels on QB toes. Split the QG and QT
Y	Head even with hip of center. 2 ft splits
B	**Split A and QT off the ball**
QT	Head even with hip of center. 2 ft splits
QG	Head even with hip of center. 2 ft splits
C	On Ball
SG	Head even with hip of center. 2 ft splits
ST	Head even with hip of center. 2 ft splits
Q	Heels at 5 yards

Red
Flex

(X) (QT) (QG) [C] (SG) (ST) (Y)

(A) (B)

(F) (Q)

Position	Alignment
X	Top of the numbers
A	Split X and QT off the ball
F	Heels on QB toes. Split the QG and QT
Y	**6 yards outside of B on line of scrimmage**
B	2x2 off ST
QT	Head even with hip of center. 2 ft splits
QG	Head even with hip of center. 2 ft splits
C	On Ball
SG	Head even with hip of center. 2 ft splits
ST	Head even with hip of center. 2 ft splits
Q	Heels at 5 yards

Blue
Flex

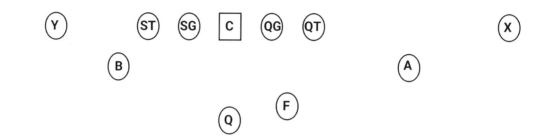

Position	Alignment
X	Top of the numbers
A	Split X and QT off the ball
F	Heels on QB toes. Split the QG and QT
Y	**6 yards outside of B on line of scrimmage**
B	2x2 off ST
QT	Head even with hip of center. 2 ft splits
QG	Head even with hip of center. 2 ft splits
C	On Ball
SG	Head even with hip of center. 2 ft splits
ST	Head even with hip of center. 2 ft splits
Q	Heels at 5 yards

Red
Empty Flop

Position	Alignment
X	Top of the numbers
A	**On numbers to the strong side**
F	**Split QT and X off the ball**
Y	Head even with hip of center. 2 ft splits
B	2x2 off Y
QT	Head even with hip of center. 2 ft splits
QG	Head even with hip of center. 2 ft splits
C	On Ball
SG	Head even with hip of center. 2 ft splits
ST	Head even with hip of center. 2 ft splits
Q	Heels at 5 yards

Blue
Empty Flop

Position	Alignment
X	Top of the numbers
A	**On numbers to strong side**
F	**Split QT and X off the ball**
Y	Head even with hip of center. 2 ft splits
B	2x2 off Y
QT	Head even with hip of center. 2 ft splits
QG	Head even with hip of center. 2 ft splits
C	On Ball
SG	Head even with hip of center. 2 ft splits
ST	Head even with hip of center. 2 ft splits
Q	Heels at 5 yards

Red
Mustang

X   QT   QG   C   SG   ST   Y

A

F   B

Q

Position	Alignment
X	Top of the numbers
A	Split difference between X and QT
F	Split QT and X off the ball
Y	Head even with hip of center. 2 ft splits
B	**Heels on toes of QB split the ST and SG**
QT	Head even with hip of center. 2 ft splits
QG	Head even with hip of center. 2 ft splits
C	On Ball
SG	Head even with hip of center. 2 ft splits
ST	Head even with hip of center. 2 ft splits
Q	Heels at 5 yards

Blue
Mustang

   C

Position	Alignment
X	Top of the numbers
A	Split difference between X and QT
F	Split QT and X off the ball
Y	Head even with hip of center. 2 ft splits
B	**Heels on toes of QB split the ST and SG**
QT	Head even with hip of center. 2 ft splits
QG	Head even with hip of center. 2 ft splits
C	On Ball
SG	Head even with hip of center. 2 ft splits
ST	Head even with hip of center. 2 ft splits
Q	Heels at 5 yards

Red
Mustang Flop

X   QT   QG   C   SG   ST   Y   A

F   Q   B

Position	Alignment
X	Top of the numbers
A	**On numbers to strong side**
F	Split QT and X off the ball
Y	Head even with hip of center. 2 ft splits
B	**Heels on toes of QB split the ST and SG**
QT	Head even with hip of center. 2 ft splits
QG	Head even with hip of center. 2 ft splits
C	On Ball
SG	Head even with hip of center. 2 ft splits
ST	Head even with hip of center. 2 ft splits
Q	Heels at 5 yards

Blue
Mustang Flop

Position	Alignment
X	Top of the numbers
A	**On numbers to strong side**
F	Split QT and X off the ball
Y	Head even with hip of center. 2 ft splits
B	**Heels on toes of QB split the ST and SG**
QT	Head even with hip of center. 2 ft splits
QG	Head even with hip of center. 2 ft splits
C	On Ball
SG	Head even with hip of center. 2 ft splits
ST	Head even with hip of center. 2 ft splits
Q	Heels at 5 yards

Adding Formations

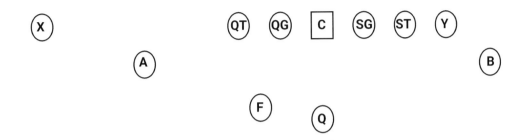

This system is designed to allow the coach the ability to get into multiple formations. We would simply add a "tag" for a formation to the player that is moving. At the high school level, we would like to be able to run many looks, but we want to play fast. This causes us to limit formation each game to 3-4 base looks. While we **CAN** get into any look, we don't always feel the **NEED** to do so.

Again, at the youth level I would recommend picking 3-4 formations at most and sticking with those formations. This will allow more time to work on fundamentals and timing.

Power of Formations

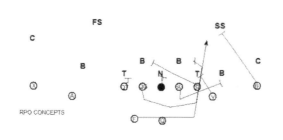

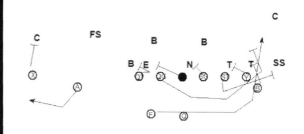

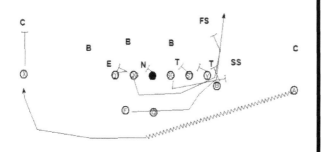

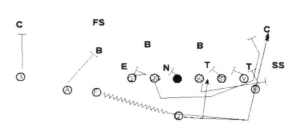

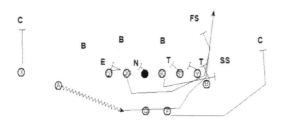

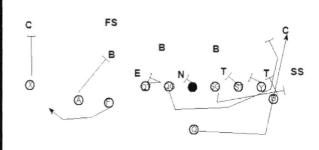

This is Buck Sweep run from multiple formations and from multiple motions. I use this as simply and example of why formations and motions matter in this offense. Running the base play is most important, but being able to motion and use formation gives a great advantage.

Motions/Shifts

Motions/Shifts

Motions are difficult to get work with the timing in a shotgun system. We generally **DO NOT** use motions until around the 6th grade. If we want to run Jet sweep we will simply cheat our "B" closer to the ball.

Each team is different, so I wanted to share the motions in this section, but this needs to only be installed after the players are comfortable with the base offense and formations.

Bus

B flat motion in front of QB
If run play, ball snapped before B crosses the QB
If pass play, ball snapped after B crosses the QB

Red

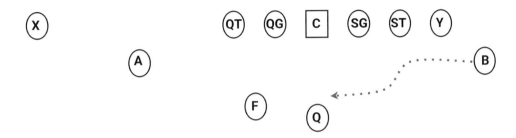

Blue

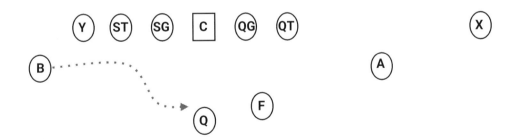

Train

A Motion
From normal, ball snapped at QT
F automatically goes to Strong

Red

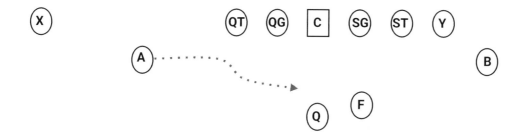

Blue

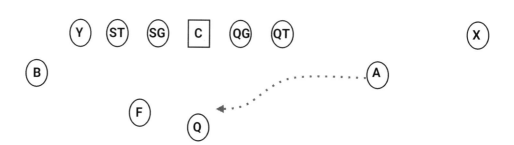

Train

A Motion
From flop, ball snapped behind QB

Red Flop

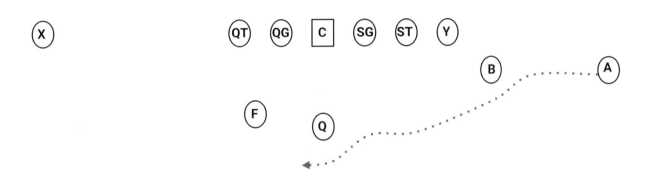

Blue Flop

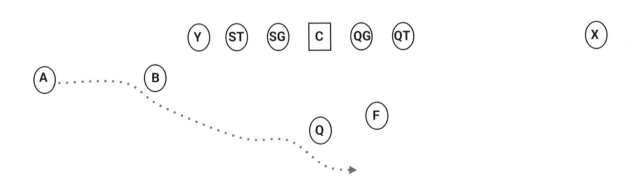

Fly

F Motion
Going out towards sideline
Ball snapped after he gets 3 steps

Red

X   QT QG C SG ST Y

A   B

F   Q

Blue

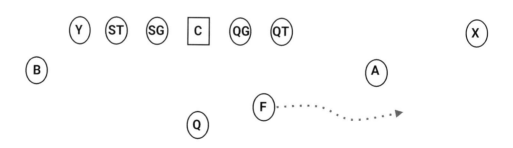

Y ST SG C QG QT   X

B   A

       F

Q

Fly

F Motion
From Empty snapped before crossing QB

Red Empty

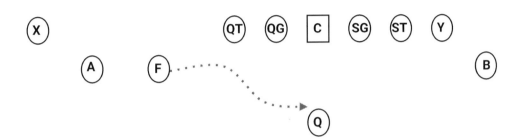

Blue Empty

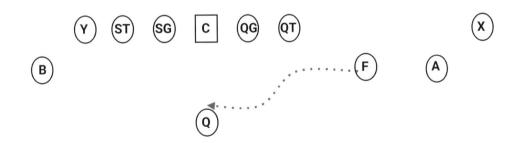

PLAYS

Buck Sweep

Buck Series Overview

The beauty of the Wing-T is series-based offense. The buck series of this offense includes the following plays:

-Buck Sweep
-Counter
-Waggle
-Buck Pass

The goal of each play is to look the same in the backfield. That is the point of series football, and something I have strived to keep true in the Gun T RPO system.

What I believe makes this system unique is that this system also has RPO's built in off the buck sweep and the counter game. Each play is part of a series, but is also run as a stand-alone with built in answers.

Buck
Base Rules

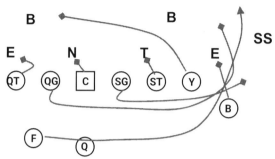

Position	Job Description
X	
A	
F	Cross QB's face for 2 steps, find quick guard and get hand on his back
Y	Gap/Down/Backer
B	Gap/Down/Backer
QT	Step Hinge or Cut
QG	Pull Wrap
C	On/Backside
SG	Pull Kick
ST	Gap/Down/Backer
Q	

Buck
Base Rules

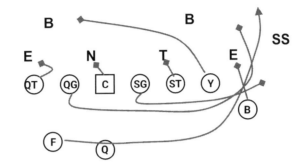

Terms –

Gap – Defensive Linemen Playing Inside Gap
Down – Defensive Lineman Playing Head Up Inside Player
Backer – Go to the Inside Linebacker

Gap-Hinge – Protect the inside gap and then hinge to pick-up the outside player

Pull Kick – Flat pull to kick the first defensive player on edge

Pull Wrap – Gain depth and work up-field to inside linebacker

4-3

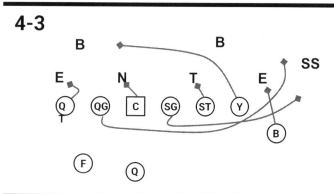

4-2

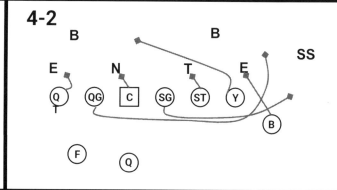

Under

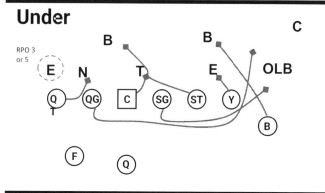

5-2

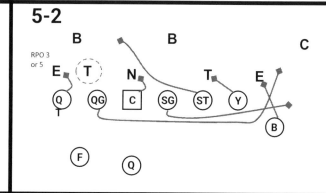

3-3

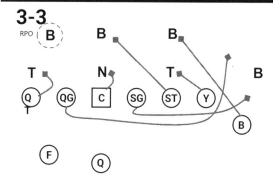

Stay Call= A & B gaps covered or 3

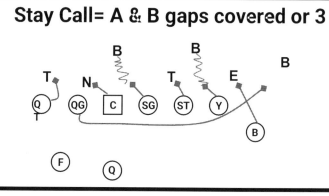

"Bypass"
Tells B leave the 9
Kick out on 9

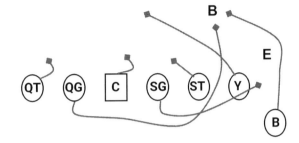

"Dubs"
Tells Y and B to double team
Y vertical push
B horizontal push
Work to backside backer

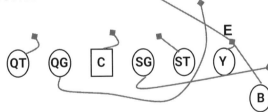

"Stay"

A and B gaps covered or threatened

C and SG block Down

QG has kick out

RPO's off Buck

"Steal"

QB reads the 4i/3 tech

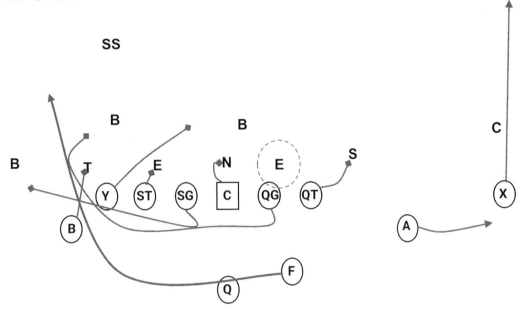

"Key"

Can throw fast screen (A steps on toes of "X" and blocks
Most Dangerous). Post snap QB reads ILB for a run

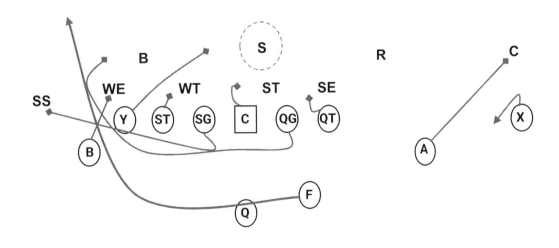

RPO's off Buck

"Read and Bogo"

QB reads the 5 tech. Can throw bubble post snap

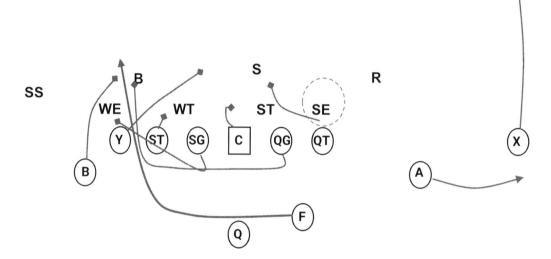

Flavors of Buck

Red-Over-Train-Buck

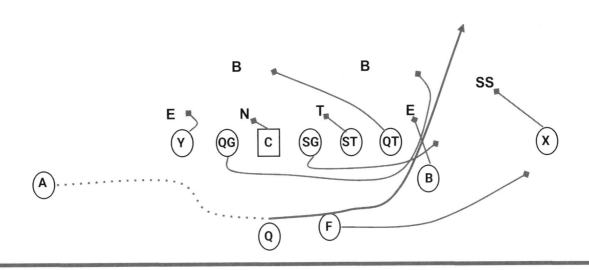

Red-Empty-Q Buck-Fast

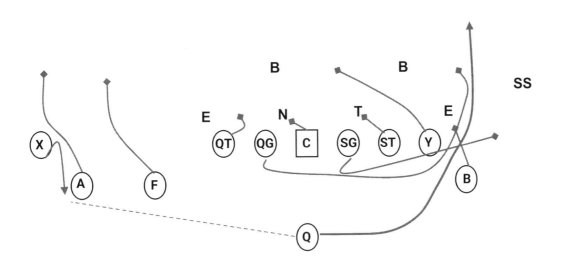

Flavors of Buck

Blue-Buck-Bubble

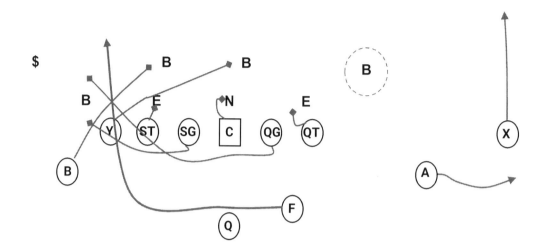

Blue-Bus-Q-Buck

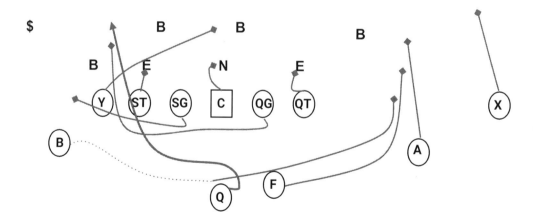

Belly

Belly Series Overview

Belly is independent from series, since the backfield action is different than the buck sweep. However, we pair it with the same play-action game and RPO's from Buck Sweep.

The goal of Belly is to give an inside run that will be a simple install and look the same in the backfield as Buck.

Belly
Base Rules

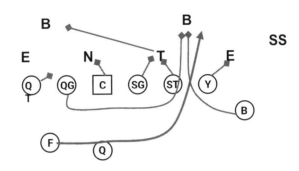

Position	Job Description
X	
A	
F	Slide step to the QB, attack downhill behind pulling guard
Y	Block out
B	Fold inside to playside LB
QT	Step-hinge unless RPO
QG	Wrap to first daylight. Eyes inside
C	On/Backside
SG	#1 Defensive Lineman
ST	#2 Defensive Lineman. If #2 is outside Y, then DBL to backside LB
Q	

Belly
Base Rules

DS   FS

BC   FC

SS

B   B

E   N   T   E

X   Q   QG C SG ST Y

A   B

F   Q

Blocking on this play is to "base" out – or turn out on players and push them to the side. Simple blocking scheme is what makes it very adjustable.

The play can hit in "A, B or C" gap depending on the defensive alignment.

We will number off the blocking on first level defenders (or defensive linemen). Center has "on-backside" Guard has #1. Tackle has #2 (unless he is outside the Y). Y blocks out.

Often, our Guard will end up with a double team with either the center or the tackle.

B will look for first threat and first open gap based on the defensive alignment.

QG will wrap to first daylight – he may end up in a different gap than the B and that is fine. He generally blocks backside/middle linebacker.

Belly

4-3

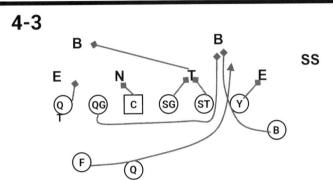

4-2

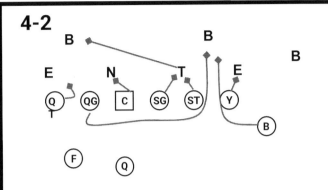

Under

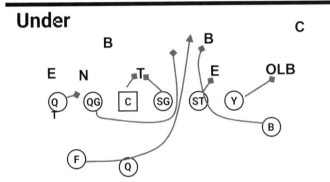

5-2

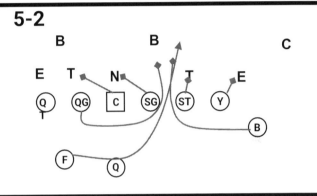

3-3

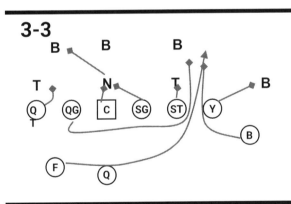

"Fan" Tells wing to block OLB

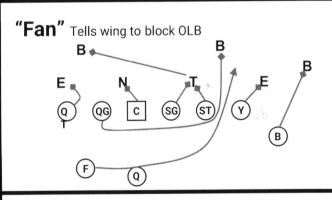

"Switch" If wide OLB, Y and B can switch

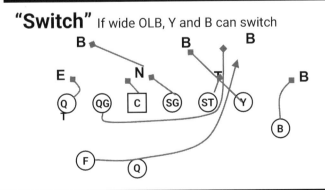

Flavors of Belly

Red-Empty-Q Belly-Fast

QB Reads #'s to trips side. A blocks most
dangerous. F blocks number 2.

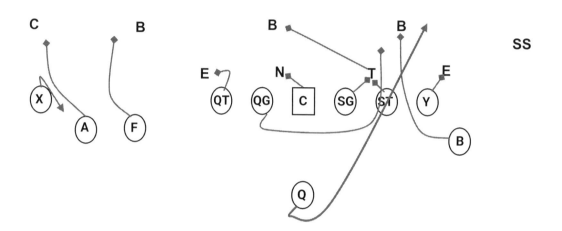

Red-Flop-Belly

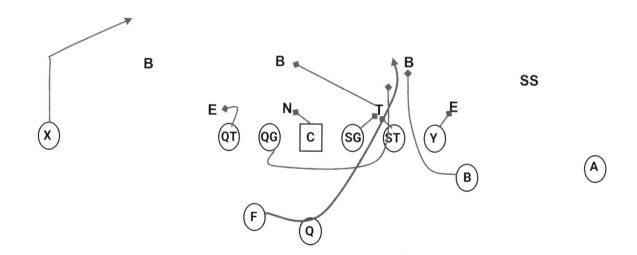

Flavors of Belly

Blue-Bus-Belly

Q fake to B, hand to F

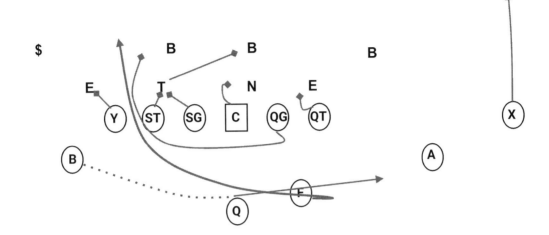

RPO's off Belly

"Read and Bogo"

QB reads the 5 tech. Can throw bubble post snap

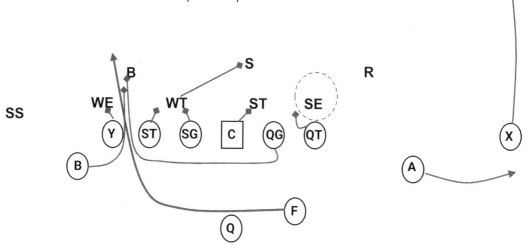

"Key"

Can throw fast screen (A steps on toes of "X" and blocks
Most Dangerous). Post snap QB reads ILB for a run

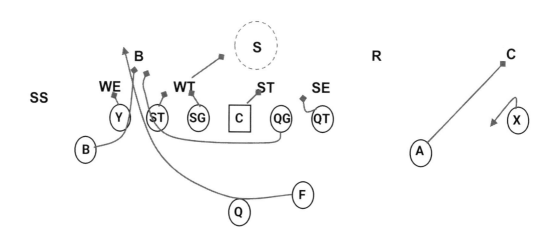

RPO's off Belly

"Steal"
QB reads the 4i/3 tech

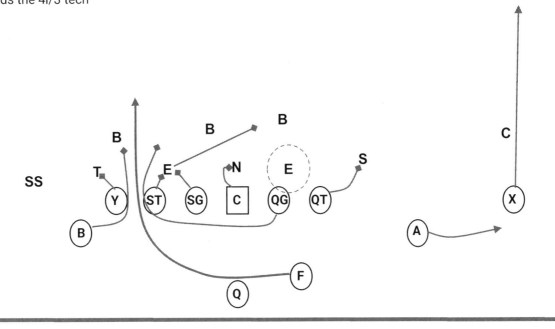

Counter

Counter Overview

The counter is part of the buck sweep series. However, in the Gun T RPO system, it can also be run with built-in RPO's on both sides of the field. The ability to run it as old-school misdirection is dangerous, but to run it with RPO's as well makes it deadly.

Teach this play the base way first as a great compliment to all strong side run plays. After you are comfortable with the double handoff, the "flavors of counter" really give you a ton of options.

Counter
Base Rules

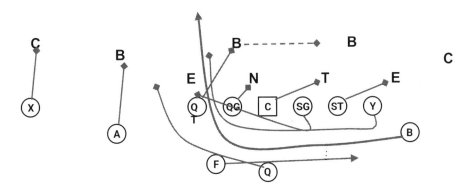

Position	Job Description
X	Block #1
A	Block #2
F	"Take" ball and give underneath carry out fake
Y	Pull Wrap
B	Counter and depth step, get ball under F
QT	Gap/Down/Backer- Work path, if playside backer flys out, don't chase, take backside
QG	Gap/Down/Backer
C	Gap/Down/Backer
SG	Pull Kick
ST	Step Hinge
Q	Give ball and block edge

Counter
Base Rules

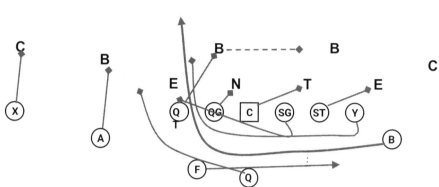

Blocking on counter is as simple as we can make it.

Our Quick side of the line to Center will block Gap-Down-Backer.

Our Strong Guard will pull and kick the first threat.

Strong Tackle will "Gap-Hinge"

Y will pull wrap – eyes inside.

B will get the ball off a double handoff.

*If you are having issues with a double handoff this could be fake to the F and then hand the all to the B or "shuffle" it forward.

Counter

4-3

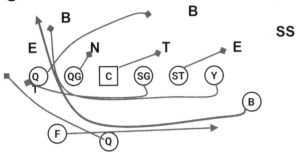

4-2

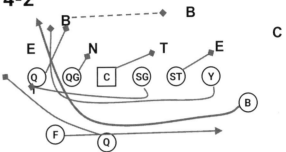

3-3

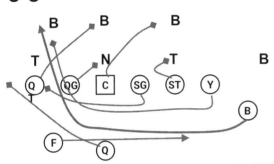

3-4

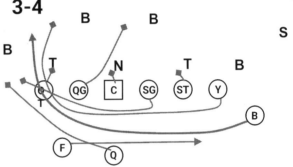

vs Blitzers

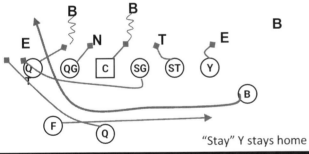

"Stay" Y stays home

Flavors of Counter

Red-Strong-Flop-Counter-Shuffle

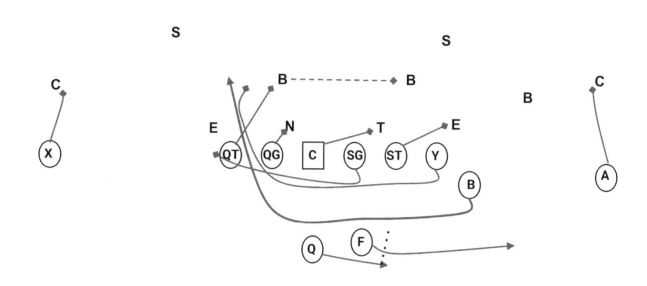

Red-Empty-Counter-43-Bubble

Bubble Presnap

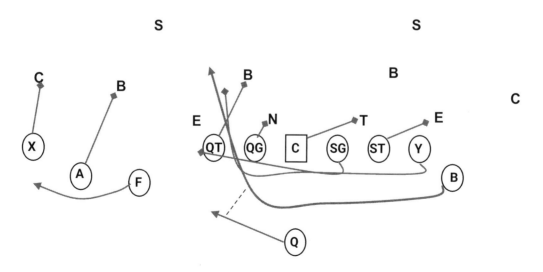

Flavors of Counter

Red-Lion-Fly-Q Counter-44 Bubble
Bubble Pre-snap

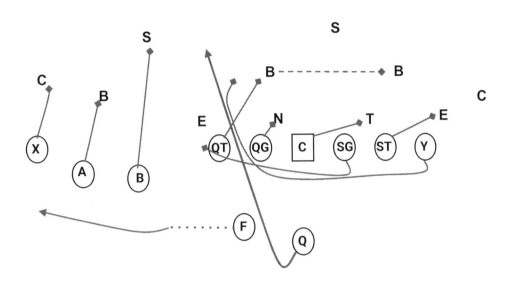

Blue-Counter-Fast
Fast Pre-snap

Flavors of Counter

Blue-Counter-Fast
Bubble Pre-snap

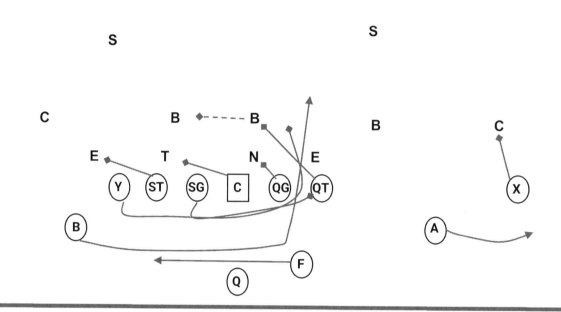

"Shuffle"
F runs option path
Q attacks edge then shuttle pass

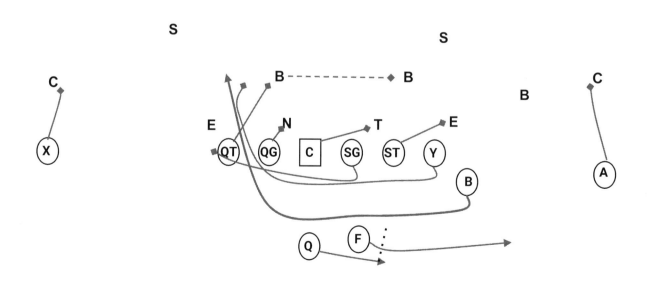

Jet

Jet Motion Overview

In keeping with the series based offense, the Gun T RPO system uses "jet motion" and marries the following plays:

-Jet Sweep
-Quick Belly
-Trips Passes
-Throwback Pass
-F Draw

This attacks the defense in every place with the same backfield action. The jet motion is difficult to adjust to as the offense transitions quickly into a 3 x 1 look. Then with the different run-pass plays built into the offense, it becomes very difficult for the defense to stop.

Each play can be run independently from the motion, but when you pair them together it gives a much more "series like" approach that is difficult to defend.

Jet
Base Rules

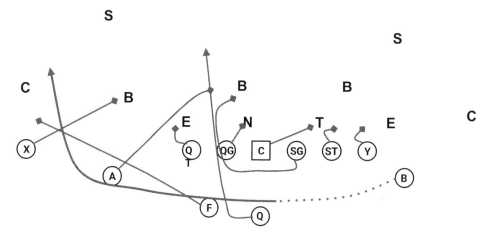

Terms –

Crack – WR will block first 2nd level defensive player inside.

Reach – Working to get to outside shoulder of the defensive player.

4-3

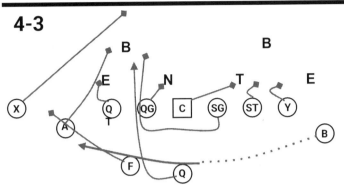

4-2

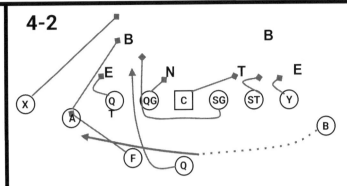

3-3 Wider splits if no 5

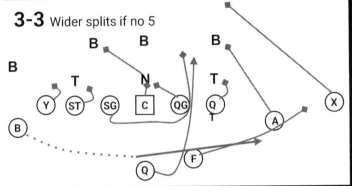

3-4

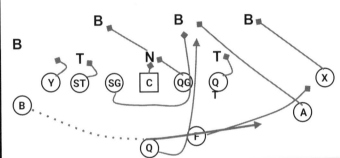

Tite

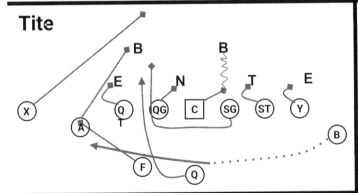

Flavors of Jet

Red-Q Jet

Q ball at chin like pass
B step hinge

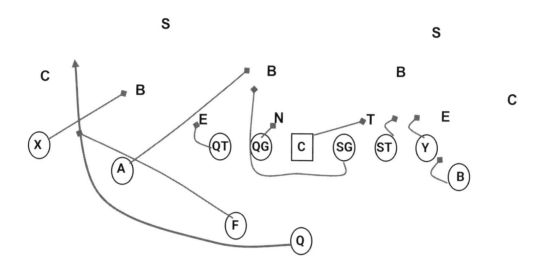

Red-Lion-Q Jet

B block ILB, chip 5 if needed. A Block OLB
X Crack Safety
Q ball at chin like pass

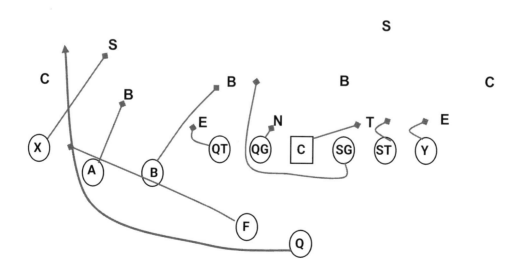

Flavors of Jet

Red-Lion-F toss-Jet

B must kick now. F toss=inside most receiver kicks

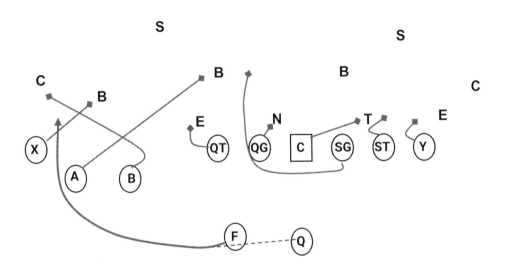

Blue-Strong-F Jet

F jet=inside receiver kicks
A kick out

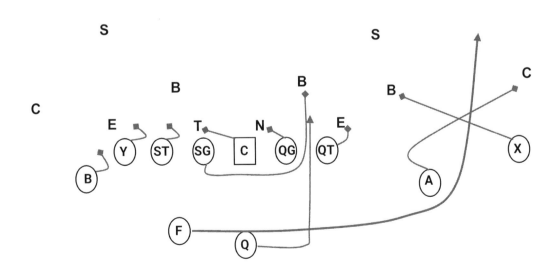

Flavors of Jet

Blue-Empty-Flop-Train-Jet
Motion on QB, follow block by F

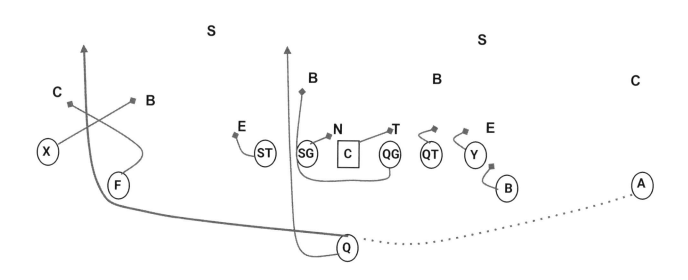

Red-Empty-Bus-Jet

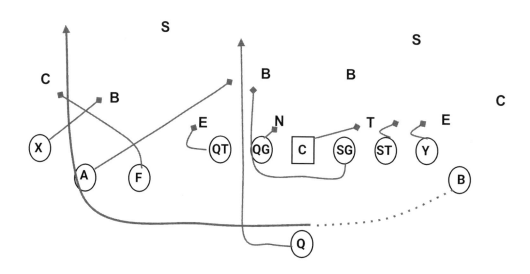

Quick Belly

Quick Belly
Base Rules

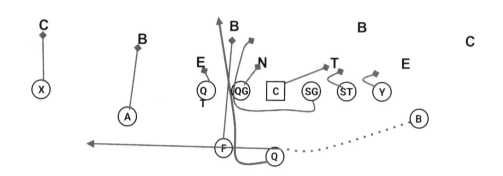

Position	Job Description
X	RPO if no motion. If motion block #1
A	RPO if no motion. If motion block #2
F	Lead on ILB (Play side)
Y	Step in, hinge
B	If motion, fake jet. No motion, step hinge
QT	#2 DL Block out, if aligned inside, take in
QG	#1 DL
C	On/Backside
SG	Wrap first gap quick side, look inside
ST	Step in, hinge
Q	Slide step, and get downhill

Quick Belly
Base Rules

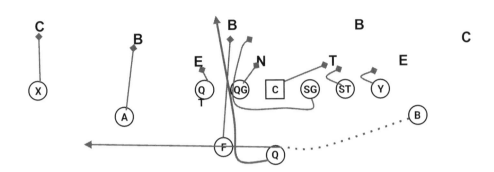

Blocking on quick belly is simply reversed from belly.

Center is on-backside. QG has #1 DL and QT has #2 DL. SG will pull wrap and our F Will lead.

This play **can be done without motion** from the B as a simple QB lead play.

Often, we will run this from a trips look and run a bubble screen on the same side.

4-3

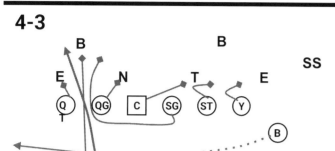

4-2

3-3 QT take where he wants to go

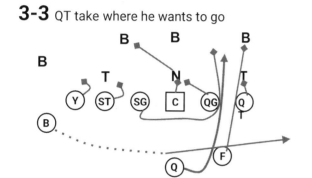

3-4

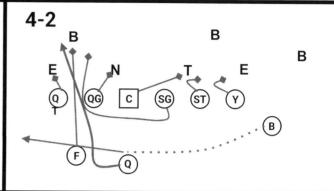

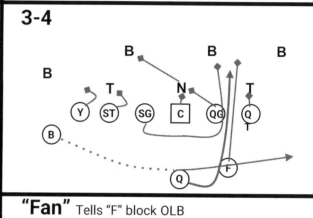

Tite

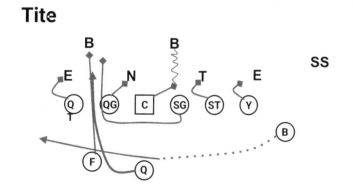

"Fan" Tells "F" block OLB

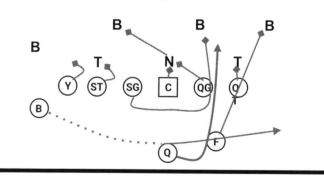

Flavors of Quick Belly

Red-Bus-Quick Belly

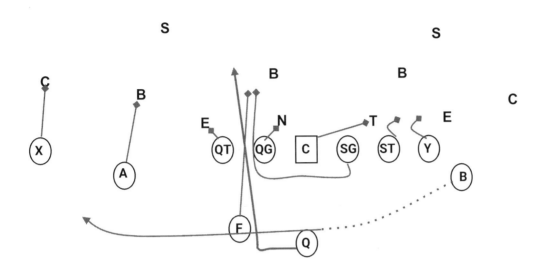

Blue-Roar-Fly-44 bubble-Quick Belly

44 bubble pre snap read

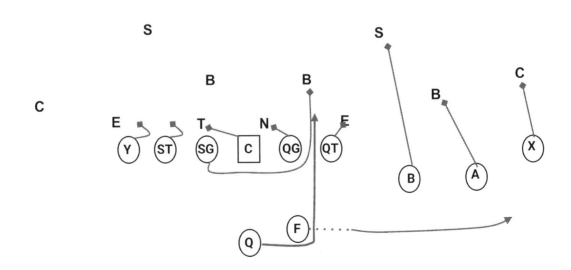

Flavors of Quick Belly

Blue-Roar-41-Quick Belly

41 Pre snap read

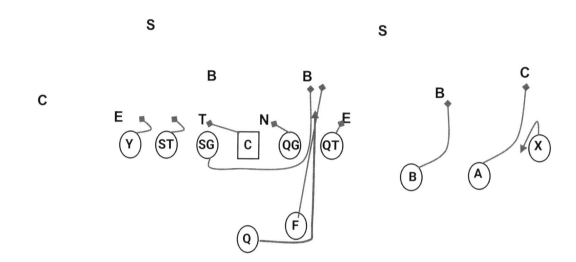

Rollout Passes

Rodeo/Lasso
Base Rules vs 4
Down

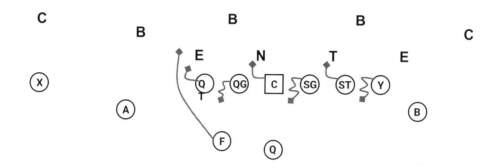

Position	Job Description
X	Route
A	Route
F	Attack outside edge, seal DE or find ILB on edge
Y	Check gap, if no pressure stay square (If not in route)
B	Route
QT	Reach end
QG	Check gap, if no pressure stay square
C	Reach 1 tech
SG	Check gap, if no pressure, hinge back
ST	Reach 3 Tech
Q	Attack edge and fit off "F" block

Rock/Load
Base Rules vs 4
Down

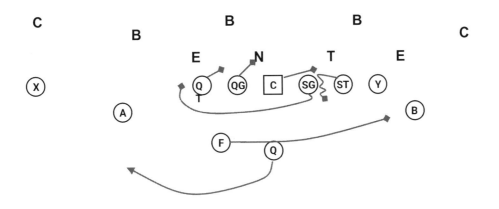

Position	Job Description
X	Route
A	Route
F	Play fake and block DE/OLB
Y	Check gap, if no pressure stay square (If not in route)
B	Route
QT	Block back, gap protect
QG	Block back, gap protect
C	Block back, gap protect
SG	Pull with depth and attempt to log
ST	Inside hinge
Q	Fake to F and roll out

Rollout Protections vs 3 Down

Rodeo/Lasso

Playside stay square. Block gap
Backside block gap, if no show hinge with depth

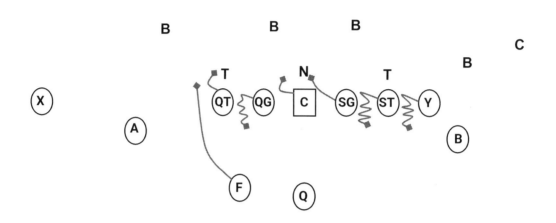

Rock/Load

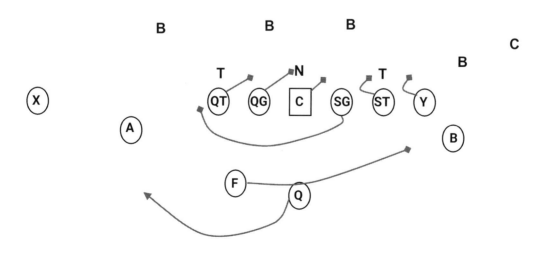

Flood

Flood

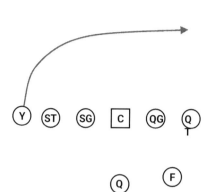

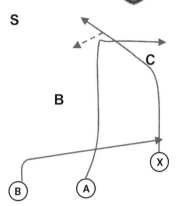

Position	Job Description
X	Skinny Post, get inside leverage on corner. If can't get over corner, turn to curl at 18
A	Smoke route, "sloppy wheel" to 16 yards, break back to 14
F	Rodeo/Lasso
Y	Drag route over LB. Choke down at hash
B	Chute route-get wide
QT	Rodeo/Lasso
QG	Rodeo/Lasso
C	Rodeo/Lasso
SG	Rodeo/Lasso
ST	Rodeo/Lasso
Q	Attack edge. Read flat defender to deep. B is hot or if flat defender drops

Snag

Snag

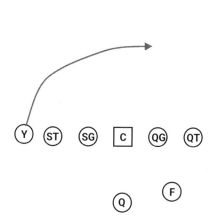

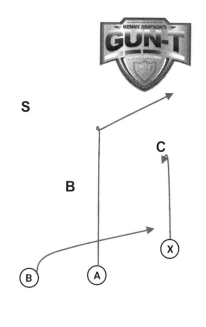

Position	Job Description
X	10-12 yards and get "clear vision lane" to QB
A	Push 7-10, aim for front pylon. QB may bend you
F	Rodeo/Lasso
Y	Drag route over LB. Choke down at hash
B	Chute route-get wide
QT	Rodeo/Lasso
QG	Rodeo/Lasso
C	Rodeo/Lasso
SG	Rodeo/Lasso
ST	Rodeo/Lasso
Q	Attack edge. Read flat defender to deep. B is hot or if flat defender drops

Rub

Rub

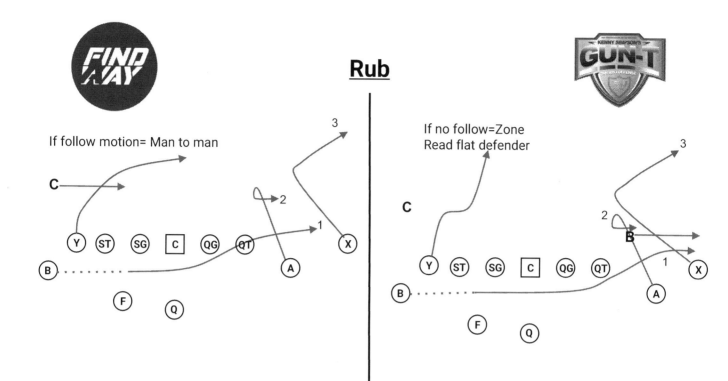

Position	Job Description
X	Tighten splits. Crack corner
A	Tighten splits. Run "In path" of man defender. Seal OLB for ball
F	Rodeo/Lasso
Y	Drag route over LB. Choke down at hash
B	Fast motion to chute route
QT	Rodeo/Lasso
QG	Rodeo/Lasso
C	Rodeo/Lasso
SG	Rodeo/Lasso
ST	Rodeo/Lasso
Q	Flat roll. Attack to run. If man, read OLB/SS for chute/stick

Play Action

Waggle
Can use Rodeo/Lasso protection

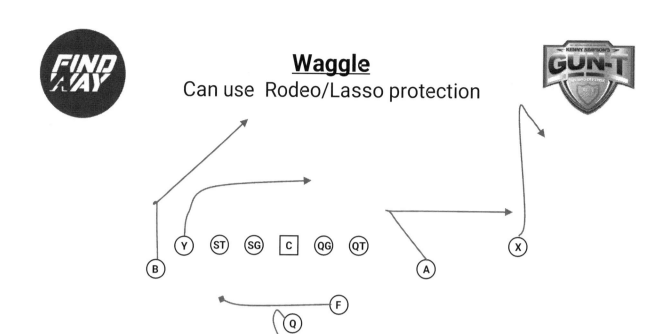

Position	Job Description
X	Smoke route. 16 yards back to 14
A	3 steps inside, break to flat
F	Fake buck and block edge
Y	Drag over linebackers
B	Post over safety
QT	Down
QG	Down
C	Down
SG	Pull and secure edge
ST	Step and Hinge
Q	Fake and shuffle, get depth. A is hot, X is primary, Y is second

Blue-Waggle-Throwback-Screen

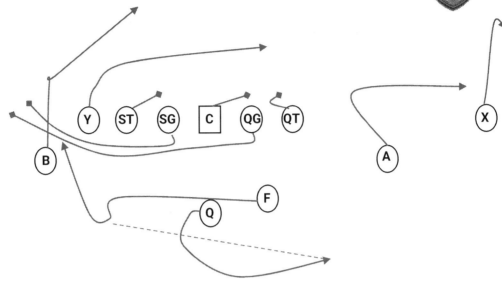

Position	Job Description
X	Waggle
A	Waggle
F	Fake buck and drift wide. Call "go" on catch
Y	Waggle
B	Waggle
QT	Buck
QG	Pull for Buck and "miss". Look inside on go call
C	Buck
SG	Pull for Buck and "miss". Block #1 on go call
ST	Buck
Q	Look like waggle and buy time. Throw to F

Buck Pass
Called if 5 tech and OLB

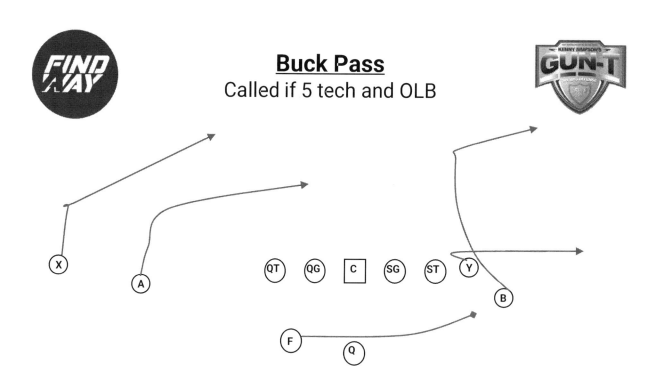

Position	Job Description
X	Post over safety. If no safety, skinny post
A	Drag over linebackers
F	Fake buck, protect edge
Y	Hands on DL for count then flat
B	Inside of OLB for release, then vert, then corner route
QT	Rock/Load
QG	Rock/Load
C	Rock/Load
SG	Rock/Load
ST	Rock/Load
Q	Flash and drop shoulder pad level as you slide step. Read deep defender for high low. If DBs "spin" work to drag

Buck Pass Y Throwback

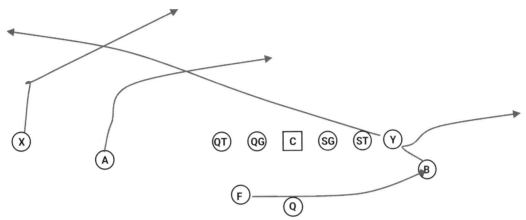

Position	Job Description
X	Tighten splits. Post over safety. If no safety, skinny post
A	Tighten splits. Drag over linebackers
F	Fake buck, protect edge
Y	Get to 15-20 yards deep across the field
B	Block down and get hands on DL for count, then release to flat
QT	Rock/Load
QG	Rock/Load
C	Rock/Load
SG	Rock/Load
ST	Rock/Load
Q	Flash and drop shoulder pad level as you slide step. Read corner to wide receiver side.

Screens

Screens Numbering System

Fast Screen

41 Fast   42 Fast   43 Fast

X

A

B F

B or F,
depending on formation

Bubble Screen

42 Bubble   43 Bubble   44
                          Bubble
                          F coming
                          out of backfield

X

A

B F

B or F,
depending on formation

Fast

System

41
Fast

42
Fast

43
Fast

X

A

B F

B or F,
depending on
formation

Blocking Rules

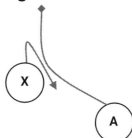

X

A

"Fast Hands"
If off coverage, gain 2
yards, turn for ball

Step on toes of "X" to
Most Dangerous

41-Fast-Lion/Roar

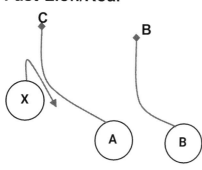

41-Fast- "X"

Prefer this against off coverage

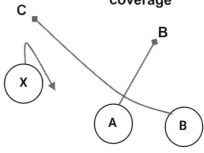

42-Fast-Lion/Roar

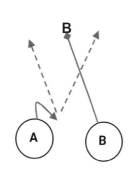

Cheat splits, read block
by B

43-Fast-Lion/Roar

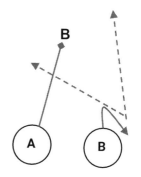

Cheat splits, read block
by A

Bubble

System

42 Bubble   43 Bubble   44 Bubble
F coming out of backfield

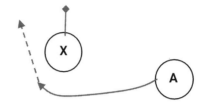

B or F, depending on formation

Block Most Dangerous   If don't catch now, go up now

Bubble

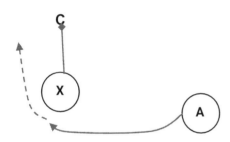

Lion-Bubble

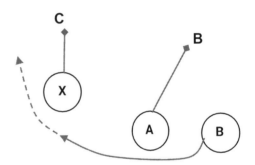

Empty Bubble

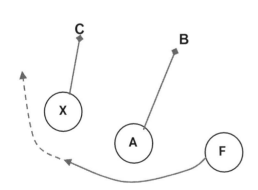

Pair with Plays

- **All Strong Runs**
- **QB Jet as an RPO**

Screens

We like to pair our screens with our run game. At the youth level we would tell the QB to throw the screen or run the ball with a signal after we are on the line of scrimmage.

As the QB progresses in the system they often can be given rules that would determine if they throw or run. Here are a few rules that would cause us to throw the screen:

1) If the numbers favor the offense – 2 WR and 1 DB
2) If the "leverage" of the Defender is bad – Too deep, too far inside

Rocket
Base Rules

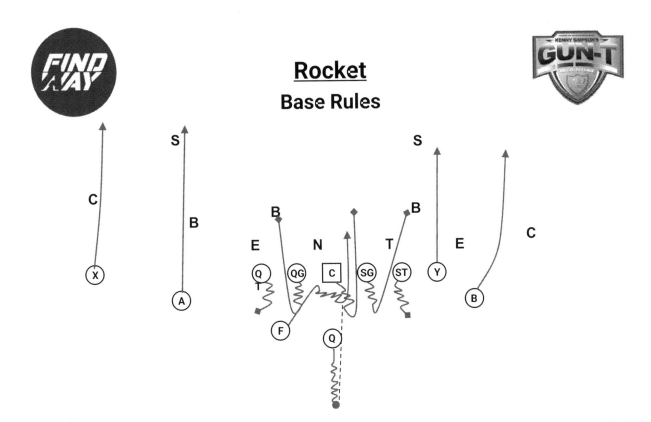

Position	Job Description
X	Go route
A	Go route
F	Step up for 2 counts, run away from any DL
Y	Go route
B	Go route
QT	Pass protect
QG	Show Pass for 1 count, then release to ILB
C	Show pass for 1 count, then release to most dangerous linebacker
SG	Show pass for 1 count, then release to ILB
ST	Pass protect
Q	Bail 3 steps and sit, then fade back to draw rush

Heavy Package

Heavy Set Overview

Using this set and these plays in the Gun T RPO offense, we are at a 90% conversion rate on 3rd/4th and short. The goal is to pick our best player and run him behind our best blockers. The goal of this set is to keep it simple and convert on short yardage.

Personnel decisions -
Strong side needs to be your best three linemen.
Keep an eligible player at the nub/"Y".
QB stays on the field if he is not the one getting the snap at the "X".
Fastest player on the team at "A".
Best players at blocking in space go to the fullback spots.

Heavy Package
Base Rules
Lineman never pull. Can be in 4 pt
stance. F and B can be personnelled

S

S

C

B   B   B

B   C

E   N   T   E

(Y) (QG) [C] (SG) (ST) (QT)   (X)

(F) (B)

(A)

(Q)

Position	Job Description
X	On line of scrimmage. Often is the QB
A	Off line of scrimmage
F	2 ft back between SG and ST
Y	On line next to QG
B	2 ft back between ST and QT
QT	On line next to ST. Can 4 pt stance
QG	On line next to C. Can 4 pt stance
C	On ball
SG	On line next to C. Can 4 pt stance
ST	On line next to SG. Can 4 pt stance
Q	Often is best athlete. Normal depth

Power

Position	Job Description
X	Block #1
A	Block #1
F	Wrap to inside backer
Y	Down block
B	Kick end
QT	Down block
QG	Down block
C	Down block
SG	Down block
ST	Down block
Q	Follow F up the hole

Train Power

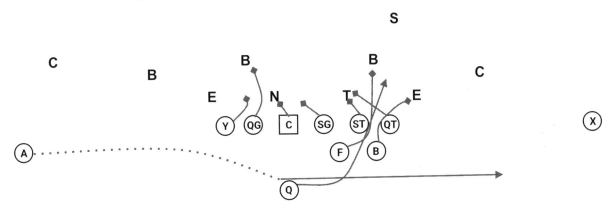

Position	Job Description
X	Block #1
A	Train motion, fake jet
F	Wrap to inside backer
Y	Down block
B	Kick end
QT	Down block
QG	Down block
C	Down block
SG	Down block
ST	Down block
Q	Fake jet to A, run power

Counter

Position	Job Description
X	Block #1
A	Block #1
F	Kick back side end
Y	Down block
B	Wrap to backside backer
QT	Down block
QG	Down block
C	Down block
SG	Down block
ST	Down block
Q	Fake power for 1 step, follow F and B

Belly

Position	Job Description
X	Block #1
A	Block #1
F	Climb to backer
Y	Down block
B	Climb to backer
QT	Kick outside
QG	Down block
C	Down block
SG	Block #1
ST	Block #2
Q	Follow B up the hole

Train Jet

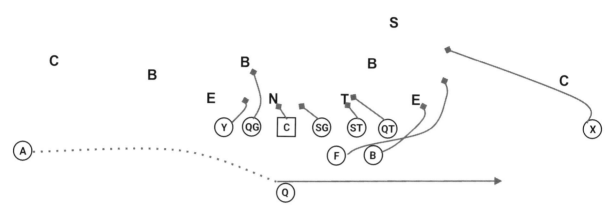

Position	Job Description
X	Crack safety
A	Train motion, take jet, follow second up man
F	Log the DE
Y	Down block
B	Log the DE
QT	Down block
QG	Down block
C	Down block
SG	Down block
ST	Down block
Q	Give the jet to A

Train Reverse Pass

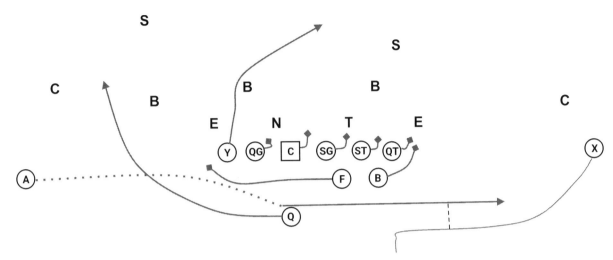

Position	Job Description
X	Take ball on reverse, look for Y first, Q second
A	Train motion, take jet, hand to X on reverse
F	Log the DE backside
Y	Banana route behind backers
B	Log the DE
QT	Pass pro
QG	Pass pro
C	Pass pro
SG	Pass pro
ST	Pass pro
Q	Give the jet to A, run wheel route

Practice Organization

Practice Organization

This is a general practice plan we have for installation. We work a "series" during individual time, then the passes off that series in periods 15-16, then the run attached during inside period. For example, if we were working our "belly series" we would cover an RPO attached during individual/pod and team. During pass period we would work quick game, or the screens attached.

There are more practice plans later in the book, but this is our general formatting. We would also steal time in period ¾ for the OL/QB for any explaining that needed to take place.

PD	QB	T	Y/B	X and A	OL	DL	ILB	OLB	DB	
1	SPECIALTY PERIOD --- DC with Non-specialty defensive players --- OL Coach with all linemen not involved									
2	Coach With Kicker, Coach With PAT Group, Coach With Punter/Snapper, Coach With Returnmen									
3	SPECIAL TEAMS GROUP - ROTATE THROUGH MAIN 4 -- Steal time for QB/OL -- Steal time for DL/ILB or DB/OLB									
4										
5										Crossover
6										
7	BREAK					BREAK				
8										Indy/Pod
9										
10										
11										
12	BREAK					BREAK				
13	1's on 1's - 5 minute offense vs. our defense, 5 minute offense working cards									1 on 1s
14										
15	1 on 1's PASS PERIOD					1 on 1's INSIDE PERIOD				
16										
17	BREAK PERIOD					DEFENSIVE PERSONELL GROUPINGS				Defense groupings
18	OFFENSIVE PERSONNELL OR SPECIALS					BREAK PERIOD				Offense groupings
19	Situational Offensive Period (TEAM)					Situational Defensive Period				Vs. Scout group
20										
21										
22	BREAK									
23	CONDITIONING									
24										

Practice Organization

All practices need to contain at least 3 elements:

-Individual time: Working on specific skills and developing each player.

-Group time: Smaller groups (I will go in detail on how we use "PODS" and Inside/7 on 7 later) to work on timing.

-Team time: This is where each team must practice the situations of the game.

In the practice schedule below, we worked our senior and junior high together. This may give you a template of working multiple teams at the same time.

The idea is to make sure the main drills are being taught and you are maximizing time. In our opinion practices should **never go over 2 hours** and should include plenty of breaks.

Time	PD	QB	F and B	Y	X and A	OL	DL	ILB	OLB	DB
	1	Senior High Special Teams				Junior High Tackling				
	2									
	3	Senior High Blocking Circuit				Junior High Special Teams				
	4									
	5	BREAK PERIOD								
	6	FTWK	FTWK	W/ OL		Indy	Jh:Off ball	JH: Agilities		JH: FTWK
	7	Tracks	Tracks	W/ OL		Indy	Jh: Stunts	JH: Horse	JH: 3 F's	JH: Ball
	8	Routes	Ball Drill	W/ WR	Routes	Indy	Jh: Read	JH: Keys	JH: Keys	JH: KEYS
	9	JH: FTWK	JH: FTWK	JH: W/ OL		JH: INDY	Off Ball	Agilities		FTWK
	10	JH: Tracks	JH: Tracks	JH: W/ OL		JH: INDY	Stunts	Horseshoe	3 F's	BALL
	11	JH: Routes	JH: Ball Dr	JH: W/ WR	JH: Routes	JH: INDY	Read	Keys	Keys	KEYS
	12	BREAK PERIOD								
	13	GROUP PERIOD: ROTATE DAYS								
	14	JH: Defensive Hip Drill / DL on Sled				SH: Blocking Circuit with OL / Skill working series				
	15	BREAK PERIOD								
	16	GROUP PERIOD: JH:								
	17									
	18	BREAK PERIOD								
	19	JH: OFFENSIVE TEAM				SH: DEFENSIVE TEAM				
	20									
	21									
	22	SH: OFFENSIVE TEAM				JH: DEFENSIVE TEAM				
	23									
	24									

Practice Organization

Picking a scout team defensive coordinator needs to become an area of importance. This coach needs to motivate and align many players that may not be very excited to practice.

Individual time does not need to always be "high in tempo". It can be slowed down to make sure everyone understands the goals. The goal is quality of quantity of reps (especially early in the year).

Don't limit your scout team to only the predicted look, be sure to work multiple fronts each week so you are always prepared. Spend 90% of the time on the prediction, but be ready. It is wise to work plays against dummies or bags early and teach the RULES, not who to block.

Work to teach the athletes to base rules of the playbook not just what you think you will see. This will take time at first, but will pay off in the long run. It is easy to move too quickly and your athletes will get confused when they see different looks. Teaching the rules helps long-term.

Installation

The Gun T RPO system is a "series based" offense. That means that each play builds off of each other. This is very much in the Wing-T world. It also has much of its roots in the RPO world. The goal is to make one play concept many by blending them together. This makes installing the Gun-T not as difficult as many of the play concepts build and steal from each other.

To begin installing, you must decide how much time your team has until the first game. Working backwards, I'd recommend 2-3 weeks to get the basic plays and RPO system installed. In this section I will share how I had 5-weeks until our first game at my most recent job. This forced a very speedy installation.

My recommendation would be to install the system out of the base set, before working formations/shifts. This allows for focus on the basics. In the next segment I will share a practice schedule form that shows our basic practice plan. We will work on rotating which "series" we are installing that day – usually by the day of the week.

Installation

Series that need to be installed:

1) Buck series
        -Buck
        -Counter
        -Waggle
        -Buck Pass

2) Belly series
        -Belly
        -RPO Game
        -Any Influence game or "no pull runs"

3) Jet series
        -Jet
        -Quick Belly
        -Rollout Passing Game
        -Draw (Belly)

RPO's and Quick game work for Buck/Belly and can be installed day 1. As you read through this guide you will see that most RPO's only involve the QB/QT and WR's.

I'd recommend working different days of the week on each. Also pairing Jet Series with any Trips game helps speed along the passing concepts.

Installation

At my most recent school, I had about five weeks to get our offense installed. The following pages are our first seven practice goals and what I was focusing on for each position group.

Each school can be different as far as a timeline is concerned. The main goal is to attempt to become great at the base plays/concepts and work to rep them as many times as possible.

New wrinkles are great, and we work to add them in as quickly as our athletes can handle them. However, we must be great at the basics first. As coaches we must constantly adapt to how quickly our athletes can handle concepts.

My advice would be to go slower than you think you must. It is always easier to come back later and add simple adjustments then to have to re-teach a basic concept that is a foundational piece.

*By the end of the seven days we were able to:
1) Line up in most of the formations I planned to run
2) Each position knew his tag to motion
3) Run all our base run plays and RPO game concepts
4) Had much of our quick game, screen game and play action game installed

*At the youth level this could be done over early season practices in smaller increments if needed.

Installation

Day 1 -
Formation period and rules - Red/Blue (flop, empty)
Motion period - "Fly"
Base run play - Buck
RPO/Screen - Fast Screen
Play Action - Waggle
QT - Base and "Steal"
OL - Buck, Rock/Load

Day 2 -
Formation period and rules - Red/Blue (Roar/Lion)
Motion period - "Bus"
RPO/Screen - Bubble
Base run play - Jet and Quick Belly
Play Action - Buck Pass
QT - Q Belly and Jet difference
OL - Quick Belly, Rodeo/Lasso

Day 3 -
Formation period and rules - Multiples (Empty-Flop and Flex-Flop)
Motion period - "Train"
Base run play - Strong Belly
RPO/Screen - Peak
Play Action - Waggle
QT - Base and Read
OL - Belly, Rock/Load

Installation

Day 4 -
Formation period and rules - Red/Blue
Motion period - All
Base run play - Counter
Pass Concept - Verticals, F Slow screens
OL - Counter, Slow Screen

Day 5 -
Formation period and rules - Flop
Base run play - Buck/Counter
Play Action - Waggle and Buck Pass
Roll Out Pass – Snag or Rub
QT - Rodeo/Lasso, Jail
OL - Buck/Counter, Rodeo/Lasso, Rock/Load

Day 6 -
Formations period and rules - Empty
Motions - "Fly"
Base run play - Q Run game (buck/belly/quick belly/q jet)
QT - Steal
OL – Review

Installation

Day 7 -
Formation period - Review
Motions - "Fly"
Base run play – Review
RPO - Screens (fast/bubble)
Pass play - Roll out pass – Snag or Flood
QT - "Read"
OL - Run game review, Pass protection

*At the youth level we would probably only pick one quick game concept and one-two screens we would run. I wanted to show what we did at the high school level as some youth teams may be a little more advanced and able to handle more passing concepts or RPO concepts. The goal is to put in what the athletes can perform well.

For example – one season we had an exceptional 5th grade group that ran more of this offense than our 6th grade team. Some teams mature at different times. But do your best to NOT DO TOO MUCH! This will confuse the kids and have an adverse effect.

Installation

I have an entire section for formations in each book because I believe they give the "flavor" for the Gun-T system. With that being said, I would suggest working base plays and RPO's before working to become exotic with formations. Here is how I structure formation installation:

Red-Blue:	First week
Red-Blue Flop:	First/Second week
Red-Blue Empty:	Second week
Red-Blue Lion/Roar:	Second/Third Week
Other formations:	Fourth/Fifth Week

I start with "bus" motion the first week as well. When installing the Jet series it is natural to work this motion.

"Train" and "Fly" motion will come as you install "Flop" and "Empty" sets.

Since I was rushed to install the offense last season, you can see I worked much quicker (it also helps that I am much more comfortable with this offense). It can be sped up, but usually is best to go slow with formations.

Tempo

My goal in tempo is to be multiple. We want to have the ability to go fast pace, but also the ability to "check with me at the line". Finally, we also want to be able to "milk the clock" if needed.

The most difficult tempo is NASCAR – This must be practiced often.
Here are a few tips for NASCAR:
1) Limit formations to 1-2
2) Limit plays run to 5-6
3) Practice at end of every practice early in the season

The second tempo is "normal" for us. We want to be on the line with 20-25 seconds left on the play clock to have the ability to shift, check with me or motion.

The last tempo is our 4-minute offense. We are not in a rush, but want to be on the ball with 10 seconds on the play clock.

When coaching at any level it is important to practice fast if you want to play fast. However, remember if you move fast – the formations and plays must be limited. It would be smart to set up a 4-5 play script for NASCAR pace.

Coaching Staff

How you use your assistant coaches is key on all football staffs, but in this offense, there are a few adjustments that can be made to help if you have a large or short staff. Here are the positions that it would be optimal to have a position coach for – **in a perfect world, here is how I'd set up my staff**:

OL – 2 coaches. One coach would handle Centers and Tackles and one would handle our guards. They could work with each other during install and separate out for pod work with one coach specializing in pulls and blocking in space and the other on down blocking and first level blocks.

TE – 1 coach. This player needs to be coached as an OL and a WR.

B – 1 coach. Again, a versatile player that needs to be coached up well.

WR's – 1 coach. Can work with A and X in this offense with one coach.

QB – 1 coach. Usually, the OC or HC.

RB – 1 coach. This position can be grouped with the QB or B coach if needed.

This is the best way to organize your staff if you have enough coaches. In the next pages I will give ideas on how to work with:

6 Coaches
5 Coaches
4 Coaches
3 Coaches
2 Coaches

Coaching Staff

If you have 6 coaches on offense, here is how to order them:

OL – 2 Coaches
QB – 1 Coach
TE – 1 Coach
RB/B – 1 Coach – B can work with TE coach for blocking
WR – 1 Coach

If you have 5 coaches on the offense, here is how to order them:

OL – 2 Coaches
QB/RB – 1 Coach – Can use position coaches for RB for pod work
TE/B – 1 Coach – Can use position coaches for B for pod work
WR – 1 Coach

If you have 4 coaches on offense, here is how to order them:

OL – 1 Coach – Will use other coaches for pod work
QB/RB – 1 Coach
WR – 1 Coach
TE/B – 1 Coach

If you have 3 coaches on offense, here is how to order them:

OL – 1 Coach
QB/WR/RB – 1 Coach – Can work RB/QB with the B coach in POD work.
TE/B – 1 Coach

If you have 2 coaches on offense, here is how to order them:

Lineman/TE – 1 Coach
Skill Players – 1 Coach

Conclusion

This system is something I have come up with to provide built-in answers. Making the game clear and simple for coaches and players gives them confidence to play fast and know that no matter what look the defense gives us, we will have the ability to succeed. By blending the best of three offensive worlds, we feel we have an offensive system to give our athletes the opportunity to compete. I hope you have found some clarity in this system.

The entire system can be found on Coachtube.com:

There is also more information on my website

Feel free to reach out to me if you have any questions.

Kenny Simpson
334-549-9382
@FBCoachSimpson
FBCoachSimpson@gmail.com

 # About The Author

Coach Simpson has served at three schools as the Head Football Coach: Searcy High School, a 6A school in Arkansas in 2020. Before Searcy, he was the Head Football Coach at Southside Charter. Taking over a program that had won eight games in five seasons and had been on a 20+ game losing streak, Simpson has led Southside to the playoffs for four-consecutive seasons and won two conference titles in the past three seasons. For his efforts, he was named 4A-2 Conference Coach of the Year (2017), named to the as a finalist for Hooten's Coach of the Year (2017) and has been the All-Star Nominee for the 4A-2 (2016 and 2019). He was also selected to coach in the 1st FCA Texas-Arkansas All-Star Showdown (2021). Simpson's teams have qualified for the playoffs the past 5 consecutive seasons.

Coach Simpson wrote his first book in 2019. He has since released 9 other books. Find A Way: What I Wish I'd Known When I Became A Head Football Coach, he has been a three-time best seller on Amazon in several categories.

His offense is now run across the globe in not only the United States, but also in South America, Africa, Japan, Europe and Australia. He has helped to install the Gun-T system in many schools over the past 2-years.

Simpson has also raised over $1.5 million for Southside and has overseen several major facility projects including: New Field Turf, Expansion to Fieldhouse, Expansion to the school's home bleachers, and the addition of a press box and a new video-board.

Prior to coming to Southside, Simpson took over as Head Coach at Alabama Christian Academy in Montgomery, Alabama. During his tenure there, Simpson took over a team that had been 4-18 and led them to their first home playoff game in over 20-years. For his efforts he was named Montgomery Advertiser's All-Metro Coach of the Year as well as being voted 4A Region 2 Coach of the Year (2010). Simpson also served as the head track coach at ACA and led the girl's and boy's teams to multiple top 10 finishes in 4A.

 # About The Author

Simpson began his coaching career at Madison Academy, in Huntsville, Alabama. He served as a junior high basketball and football coach, before working into a varsity coaching role in football. He graduated from Harding University in 2003. He is married to Jamey and has three children: Avery, Braden and Bennett. The couple was married in 2001 after meeting at Harding University.

@FBCoachSimpson - Twitter
FBCoachsimpson - Facebook
FBCoachSimpson.com - Website

Made in the USA
Columbia, SC
28 October 2024

45132107R00074